Wiggling on the Altar

Confessions of an imperfect woman
in love with a perfect God.

- M. B. ROOSA -

WIGGLING ON THE ALTAR

Wiggling on the Altar - Confessions of an imperfect woman in love with a perfect God- by M.B. Roosa

© 2020 Mary Beth Roosa
ISBN 978-0-578-70381-7

mbroosa55@gmail.com

Cover Design & Illustration by James Koenig - www.freelancefridge.com

WIGGLING ON THE ALTAR

WIGGLING ON THE ALTAR

DEDICATION

This book is dedicated to my Father God who taught me, and is still teaching me, what it truly means to love. And to my earthly father, Marion R. Stout, who taught me how to laugh.

WIGGLING ON THE ALTAR

PREFACE

I am not a minister of the Gospel. I don't stand behind a pulpit and preach to the masses. But I spoon-fed my children the Word of God since as early as their conception. I do not have a Doctorate in Theology, but I'm certain that I have earned an honorary degree in "Life Experience." And most importantly – I have known the love of my Savior since the first time my mother rocked me to sleep to the tune of *"Jesus Loves Me This I Know."*

I came from a long line of Lutherans – German Lutherans to be exact. My grandfather and my uncle were both Lutheran ministers and although I never knew my grandfather, I understand that he was a powerhouse behind a pulpit.

At the age of fifteen I had a personal encounter with the Holy Spirit which changed my relationship with God forever. I began attending an evangelical church and chose to make my own public declaration of faith by being re-baptized at the age of nineteen.

By twenty, I met Jack Stevens, a Christian firefighter, and my soon-to-be husband. By thirty I lost him to a horrific accident involving his fire truck and was left to raise our four baby daughters alone.

I was devastated, broken, and hopeless. Yet, it was during that time of tremendous grief that I discovered how deep my roots were in God and His Word. God was with me. He never once left my side. Even when He was silent, I could feel His presence as if He were in the room with me. And although at times I honestly thought my life was over, God in His mercy did not leave me where I was.

Not long after that loss, I met Greg, a handsome hard-working Christian carpenter. I had four daughters. He had a daughter and a son. Together we had another daughter. I have to say that remarriage, blending two families (although a blessing) wasn't always a walk in the park. Despite it all, life has had its rewards. All seven of our children are now grown, moved out, and have their own amazing families. To top it off, I'm fairly sure they still like me.

I give God all the glory!

The fact that God could take a pretty messed up woman (me) and teach her how to hang onto the horns of the altar, is a blessing. But then to have that same woman (still me) witness God do amazing things through her daily is a testimony to His uncompromising love and His unlimited grace and mercy.

Without Him I am nothing.

...

WIGGLING ON THE ALTAR

1

Psalms 127:3 (NAS) "Behold, children are a gift from the Lord."

And no, you can't regift them.

The first commandment in the Bible was for God's people to be fruitful and multiply. It recently hit me how obedient I have been. I have seven grown children (five original and two bonus), and as of this writing I have eleven grandchildren. Although I may not have replenished the earth quite yet – I am certainly off to a good start.

In some ways, I am like Abraham (unfortunately even down to the ability to grow chin hair). Although I could never boast about having as much faith as he did, I do know where my source of faith comes from – the One and only true living God.

Raising a houseful of kids wasn't always

easy – especially in a blended family. In fact, I always laugh at the word "blended" which sounds like our family is made up of something smooth and creamy like sour cream or yogurt rather than what it truly is - a bunch of nuts. There are so many other buttons on my blender that would more accurately describe what it was like bringing two separate families together – grate, chop, and crush to name a few.

Overseeing six daughters and one son was challenging in so many ways. For example, making a meal or simply choosing a restaurant that everyone agreed upon was enough to send my head spinning. I changed my spaghetti recipe so often that I could have created a spaghetti-only cookbook.

Although I would have never had the faith to willingly strap any of them down to an altar and sacrifice them by fire to the Lord, nor was I (thank God) ever commanded to do so, there were definitely times when I felt like gluing them to the wall.

However, it was during those difficult moments when I could hear my mother's sweet gentle voice whispering oh so softly in my ear, "pay back."

Thanks, Mom.

. . .

2

Proverbs 22:6 (NAS) "Train up a child in the way he should go and when he is old, he will not depart from it."

Old, as in WAY past their teenage years.

I get distracted easily. Call it A.D.D. (Attention Deficit Disorder) or perhaps an over-stimulated cognitive function. No matter what title any number of psychologists may place on this condition it takes up way too much of my time.

For instance, at this very moment, I am having a difficult time focusing due to an annoying fly buzzing around the room. I have literally stepped away from my pad of paper, and spent up to ten valuable minutes (okay, fifteen) chasing this tiny child of Beelzebub around the room with a damp dish towel.

For all of you who believe what I'm doing is wrong – that all God's creatures have a right to live – I apologize. However, in my defense, you have no idea what I'm dealing with here. This particular housefly is demon possessed. Seriously, this devil with a hundred eyes needs deliverance. So, I am simply trying to put it out of its misery – that is, if I can ever catch it.

So now that I have shared openly with you one of my many imperfections, (and God only knows how many I really have!) can you imagine God choosing someone as rattle-brained as me to raise a brood of children who were to one day turn out normal?

My thoughts exactly.

That is the reason why I believe that trying to raise children to become healthy, productive human beings and valuable assets to society without first having a personal and intimate relationship with their Creator, is improbable – or as far as I'm concerned, impossible.

I began praying for my children before I ever conceived them. I prayed for their health. I cried out to God for their hearts to be open to Him. I even prayed for their future spouses. While they struggled to grow up and define their own lives, where to go to church, what friends were truly valuable, what career choices would be their best bet, and who their spouses would be -- I fasted and prayed all the more.

So how, you may ask, can an imperfect woman like me, filled with flaws, doubts, and insecurities raise quality children who grow into fine adults who love and honor God and others? By being honest about my own shortcomings, hanging onto the horns of the altar, fasting when prompted, praying for them daily, and continually laying them down at the foot of the cross where they belong.

As far as I'm concerned, there is no other way.

. . .

3

Proverbs 31:27 (NKJV) "She watches over the ways of her household and does not eat the bread of idleness."

She is lucky if she has time to eat at all!

When I began having children, I made the decision to be a stay-at-home mom and have a bunch of them. Today, it's practically unheard of. In the current economy, the concept of both parents working is pretty much the norm. The decision of having four or more children seems almost archaic.

However, I know there are still a few women out there who have traded in their briefcases for a diaper bag – and their dry-clean-only business suits for a spit-up-stained tank top. Some are even so brave as to homeschool their children – a monumental task I personally never added to my plate.

WIGGLING ON THE ALTAR

There were three main reasons why I chose to be a stay-at-home mom:

1) I wanted to raise my children myself.
2) Childcare costs outweighed what I was currently earning in the work field.
3) I loved listening to the weird remarks made to me by women with careers.

For instance, I had a woman once say to me: "You have so many children, you must be organized!"

My reply: "I wasn't organized before I had children, what makes you think I am organized now??"

Oh, and my favorite:

A woman, with eyebrows lifted so high on her forehead they practically disappeared beneath her bangs once asked me: "Oh? You don't work?"

Although I would have liked to smack her eyebrows right back into place, I chose to use the self-control God had given me to remain silent. The woman who said this biting remark was childless.

When I was raising my children, I was not sitting around in footie pajamas, eating chocolate chip cookie dough, and watching soap operas. Quite frankly, I was busier than a one-handed-chicken-plucker! (I apologize for the reference if a one-handed-chicken-plucker happens to be reading my book. In fact, I must add, I'm extremely impressed!)

Before my first husband went home to be with the Lord, I had four little stair-step personalities at home constantly vying for my attention. And they were quite creative in how they kept me hopping from room to room.

Here are a few examples:

They used my kitchen wall as their creative coloring canvas. They got into my feminine products and used them to wallpaper my bathroom. One of them ate sand. One preferred eating bugs. I had to literally pull pieces of cricket out of my first-born's mouth (this could explain why she is now a vegetarian). One day, one daughter who was quite normally a handful all by herself, came bounding in through the back door, grinning from ear to ear and handed me a piece of petrified doggy-doo. "Look, Mommy," she squealed, "a candy bar!"

All of this happened before the invention of antibacterial soap!

So, if you choose to work outside your home, there is absolutely no condemnation. In fact, I admire you for your tenacity and fortitude in balancing work, school, and home.

But if you do have a career outside of home please remember when encountering a stay-at-home mom, that there is no Employee of the Month award for nursing, pumping, diaper-changing, or potty training. There are no quarterly bonuses for raising a brood of children, wading through mounds of daily laundry, cleaning petrified doggie-doo off of tiny hands, or preparing meals all while trying to sneak in two minutes to make oneself presentable for the husband coming home from a long day at work.

So, if you happen to meet one of the few women who have for whatever reason made the decision to stay at home and pop out a plethora of children, do them a favor. Pat them on the back, and say, "You go, girl!"

They won't feel like smacking you at all.

. . .

4

Proverbs 31:30a (NIV) "Charm is deceptive, and beauty is fleeting…"

Mine ran like the wind!

If beauty is indeed in the eye of the beholder, I say, thank God the beholder is far-sighted. Would someone please tell me when I began looking like a Shar-Pei? I mean, seriously.

Not too many years ago I was blessed with three new grandbabies pretty much right in a row. With offspring come the inevitable Nana-holding-baby photos. Now, don't get me wrong, they are precious memories.

However, I don't look like that in the mirror. I don't. I actually have a neck in the mirror. So, what's the big deal with the photos? According to digital photography I have somehow developed enough lines on my forehead that I could screw my hat on (that is, if I wore a hat). The once-supple skin on my face now looks like a California mudslide.

You see, in my minds-eye, I don't look a day over thirty. In the mirror, more like forty-five. But in digital photos it appears that I could star in any number of zombie movies - no makeup required.

You may suggest cosmetic surgery. Have you seen even one woman on television or the big screen to whom after having cosmetic surgery doesn't look like a marionette (or worse), a ventriloquist's dummy? What exactly are they having blown into their lips? Helium?

No thank you.

Time has a way of changing us: dimming the sparkle that once brightened our eyes, adding lines where taut unblemished skin used to exist. And as you can tell, I'm none too thrilled with some of these changes. But I have to say that the worst by far is menopause. Just this morning I awoke to 58 degrees with rain outside my open kitchen window, yet I couldn't enjoy it because of a major menopausal power surge. Seriously! You could have plugged me into a socket, and I would have heated the entire house.

The Doctor recommended I take a supplement to help with the transition, but I respectfully declined. I figure that if God wanted me to take a synthetic hormone, He would have put it in chocolate, right?

But I must admit, time has created some changes that have actually been for the better – like learning to take my time instead of always being in a rush, stopping to appreciate the sunrise I used ignore on my way to work, and allowing our grandchildren to misbehave a little more than I did my own children.

So, I say, "Go ahead, time, take your best shot." I don't care if one day my jowls are sitting on my shoulders, and my neck begins pooling around my collar. It may not be pretty to the eyes of Hollywood or even the beholder, but I can always wear a turtleneck sweater. So now when I start feeling depressed about the aging process, I will look up to the heavens and thank God for my grandchildren, and then take a long walk in the sunshine and let my inner thighs get reacquainted.

Now that I think about it though, if the price is right, I may consider getting surgery on my neck after all. Who knows? If I'm lucky and the surgeon tugs hard enough, it may result in a chest-lift at no extra charge.

· · ·

5

Matthew 11:28 (NAS) "Come to Me, all who are weary and heavy laden, and I will give you rest."

Trust me, this does NOT refer to family vacations.

My sister loves road trips. It is partially due to the fact that she refuses to fly. Mind you, this is the same woman who used to live in Germany, and if my memory serves me right, she didn't get there by rowing a canoe.

As soon as we are in the car, she pops her Randy Travis gospel CD into the player and yodels all the way to the hotel. You see, my sister enjoys the "process" of going on vacation. I would rather skip the process and arrive Star Trek-style. *Beam me to San Diego, Scottie!*

Kids enjoy a road trip for about a block and a half when the inevitable "are we there yet?" begins. This can also continue for the entire trek until you reach your destination, and this is precisely why the longest we ever traveled with kids was six hours.

My husband was never crazy about the "process" either. This is because he was forced to travel with seven female bladders – one of which had been trampled underfoot by five female fetuses. He also likes to do vacations in fast motion – cramming a week of amusement parks and beaches into a forty-eight-hour time slot (and that includes traveling to and from).

I used to pack goodie bags for each of the kids which included sticker books, colored pencils, pads of paper, books, and snacks that helped the trip go smoother. If you tried this on your kids today, they would look at you like you just dragged their father out of the cave. All of this was before forty-inch flat screens with surround sound and built-in DVD players in the back seat.

Now that the kids are grown I would love to take a long enough vacation where I could arrive quickly, kick the germ-infested hotel bedspread to the corner of the room, open the windows, and allow a tropical sea breeze to wash over my heavy laden body. But until that day, I will continue onward, clinging to the knowledge and the hope that there is an eternal resting place waiting for me in heaven.

Are we there yet?

. . .

6

Philippians 2:2 (NAS) "…make my joy complete by being of the same mind, maintaining the same love, united in spirit, intent on one purpose."

This does not mean that we all like the same television programs.

I love murder mysteries. I do - so sue me. (No, please don't.) I know what half of you are thinking - how can a woman who professes to be a Christian still love murder mysteries? The other half of you, if you are being truly honest, love *Mark Harmon* – you know you do.

I enjoy watching crime fighters in movies and on television, and I like reading about them in books. I have even written a few murder mysteries of my own. No, I am not homicidal. And yes, I am horrified when I hear about real-life murders. So why do I like the fictional versions of them so much?

I love puzzles. I love creating a crime and then figuring out how to solve it. I love the process of weaving a story that eventually culminates with the good guy, who has faced impossible obstacles, getting the bad guy in the end.

Does this make me a bad person? Does this make me less of a Christian? Believe me I used to struggle with this perspective - but mostly because of judgmental people.

The beauty of being one of God's children is that He created us all uniquely different. For instance, my husband Greg loves the subject of stocks, calls, and puts. I have no idea what he's talking about, but I love his enthusiasm. Even now he is trying to explain it to me, and as I'm typing instead of listening, he is throwing his hands into the air and leaving the room.

The point I'm trying to make is that God has called us to be like-minded. This does not mean that after reading this you have to start watching *NCIS*. This means that we must all recognize the fact that despite all of our differences, we are united by one God, one death on the cross, and one eternity. We are called to love one another and not judge those who are different from us.

WIGGLING ON THE ALTAR

So even though I enjoy a murder mystery now and then, I know that my Redeemer lives, I know that He is now and will be forever victorious, and I know that I know that the bad guy gets it in the end.

. . .

1

Psalms 2:4a (NIV) "The One enthroned in
heaven laughs…"

*I mean really, with kids like us, who
wouldn't?*

The Lord has a great sense of humor. Here is
an example: I grew up a chubby kid with the
last name of Stout. I rest my case. I could end
this chapter with that sentence.

A sense of humor is vital in this life. I
can't even imagine making it through one
day without laughing about my shortcomings
(I'm also short) or raising children without a
hefty dose of humor.

My dad was the laughter guru in my life.
Whenever I pouted - and I did pout (hey, I
was the baby of the family) - he would thrust
his thumb in front of my face and say, "look
over my thumb without laughing," then make
a silly face. It was hilarious at the time and
quite effective. So, of course, I tried it once

on one of my own daughters. But instead of laughing her head off, she rolled her eyes so far back in her head she fell off the chair.

Here is an example of how humor triumphed over anger when one of my kids committed a punishable offense. One day I discovered a stick figure drawn in pencil on a white bedroom door. Since some of the girls shared the room connected to the door, and none of them confessed, I asked the Lord for wisdom.

Not long after I sat the girls down at the kitchen table, gave them each a piece of paper, and instructed them to draw me a person. My second-born daughter without realizing what I was up to, drew the exact same stick person as the one on the door. I mean, I realize she was young at the time and probably only had one stick person in her repertoire, but it was identical.

I threw my head back and laughed out loud. I laughed all the way up the stairs and the entire time I watched her wash her artwork off the door. It was a great moment in history and didn't cost me one ounce of anger.

One of my favorite sayings is this: "Don't major on the minors." I'm not sure who coined the phrase, but I know it helped me manage parenthood all those years.

For instance, I did my best to only discipline my kids for outright disobedience, not mistakes like spilling milk or breaking a glass. Keep in mind this was back in the day when you were allowed to discipline your children. Nowadays if you even threaten your child with a paddling, they will divorce you, move out, and take custody of your dog.

Nevertheless, when the same daughter in her twenties decided to dye her hair pink, I did my best to place the decision in the minor category. She had been a straight A student, didn't do drugs or alcohol, and was actually on her way to a worship school.

My husband wasn't thrilled that we would have a child who resembled a cartoon character, but after I reminded him that we should not major on the minors, he too let it slide. It was either accept it or chase the train on foot.

All in all, I have discovered that a sense of humor is essential in all relationships. We are all human, we all make mistakes, and we all need Jesus. Life is much better when we take hold of that fact, don't take life so seriously, and laugh whenever appropriate.

For example, laughing that I was a chubby kid with the last name of Stout is

WIGGLING ON THE ALTAR

NOT appropriate. I rest my case.

. . .

8

Romans 12:1 (NIV) "Therefore, I urge you, brothers (and sisters), in view of God's mercy, to offer your bodies as living sacrifices, holy and pleasing to God---this is your spiritual act of worship."

This is where the wiggling begins.

I'm not going to lie. Having a family requires sacrifice.

Here are a few of the things I had to lay down in order to have children:

1) Career: Okay, maybe that's not a good example. But jumping from job to job is kind of a career.
2) Health: The moment the doctor announced that I was pregnant, I broke out in stretch marks.
3) Vocabulary: I started calling my husband Bubba and Bobo, names you'd normally

call an infant, a toddler, or a small chimpanzee.

4) Sanity: I often wandered around the house in the middle of the night, running into walls and stubbing my toes on bed frames. Believe it or not, I once broke my toe on a waterbed.

5) Romance: Finding private moments to spend with my spouse after having children was like a scene from *Mission Impossible*. It took serious planning, synchronization of watches, and the ability to move through the house with the stealth of a CIA operative. And that was only possible on the nights we could stay awake.

6) Dreams: It's almost impossible to have dreams when you never sleep.

Things I would have sacrificed if I never had children:

1) Awe: The fact that God could take my husband and me, two ridiculously imperfect people (sorry, Bubba), and create through us a tiny human being that is miraculously created in His image, blows my mind.

2) Joy: Kids give you so much to laugh

about. Really. They are hilarious. Don't get me started!

3) Love: When you look into their tiny faces for the very first time you are overcome with a *"Grinch"* moment. No, you don't feel like boycotting Christmas (this comes much later) - your heart grows three times its size!

4) Companionship: Seven best friends.

5) Overflowing Gratitude: To a loving God who walks with me daily and hears the cries of a mother's heart in the dead of the night when no one else is around.

Whether you have a family or not, the Christian life is a life laid down. God requires us to serve others, to lay down our selfishness, our rights, and sometimes even our dreams and talents in order to allow Him to work through us.

It isn't always easy. It's kind of like building an altar, crawling on top of it, and then handing God a book of matches. It requires faith. It requires confidence in a God who is trustworthy, merciful, and loving and who made the ultimate sacrifice by sending His only Son Jesus to die on the cross in our place.

My first husband Jack understood this

concept better than anyone I have ever known. More than once he told me that he would lay down his life if only his fellow firefighters would come to know Jesus as their Lord and Savior.

At his funeral, many of them did.

...

9

Proverbs 16:9 (NIV) "In his heart a man plans his course, but the Lord determines his steps."

Then why do I keep tripping over my own two feet?

Have you ever prayed about something and God didn't answer it the way you expected? Hello! Welcome to the Kingdom of God.

Let me give you an example. Suppose you are a family of six living in a two-bedroom apartment and praying fervently that God would not only provide you with at least a three-bedroom home, but one in Colorado Springs? You live in Arizona, you are sick of the heat, and everyone knows that God lives in Colorado, (at least He did until they legalized marijuana). Would you be able to discern God's hand in your life if he answered your prayer in baby steps?

For instance, while you are praying your

husband gets a job offer that is closer to home, has better pay than his current one, and has (hallelujah) no politics. Wow! What a blessing! But wait one cotton-picking minute! We wanted to move to Colorado Springs and this job is in Phoenix. This must not be from God. This must be a ploy from the enemy!

What if *Suze Orman* showed' up one night on your doorstep and offered you a free lesson in budgeting. What if she guaranteed that if you followed her ten steps you would have your dream home in one year? Now I know this is pretty farfetched but work with me here.

Would you consider either of these things a distraction from the enemy? Would you become frustrated and quit praying for your dream to move to Colorado Springs? Or would you continue praying and trusting God that He has heard your prayer and is in the process of blessing you?

Here's a tough one - what if God's answer to your prayer is "no"?

Go ahead, sit down, and take a moment to do some deep breathing. The Lamaze technique always works for me. This one is a bit difficult to swallow, and yet if we are truly to believe God has our lives in His hands, we must trust that He knows what is best for us no matter how He answers.

Here's an example. Before I met my first husband, I was in a gospel band. We went around to different churches, the Salvation Army, and even a prison facility for youth singing songs we had written to share with people the love of Jesus.

So, of course, I began to pray that the Lord would bring me a husband who was a musician. My dream was to travel around the country to different churches leading people into worship. This had to be the will of God, right? Of course, it did. I would be doing it for Him.

I even met a wonderful Christian man who not only was quite attractive, but he played the guitar and sang, and seemed to know the Bible backwards and forward. It appeared like we hit it off right away, and I was certain that he was as interested in me as I was in him.

Even though this man seemed to be everything I had prayed for and more, and even though He had asked a friend for my phone number (more than once I might add), he never called. Was this the enemy blocking the most amazing union since Sonny and Cher? Okay – bad example.

WIGGLING ON THE ALTAR

Not long after all of this I met Jack. He was a Christian fireman who owned a guitar he didn't know how to play, loved singing, but not always in tune, and he was everything I could have ever wanted in a husband and father. There was never an inkling of doubt in my mind that God had called us together.

So, my point is this – while you are praying, fasting, and believing God for an answer to your prayer, no matter how He answers, remember God always has your best in mind.

Jeremiah 29:11 (NIV) "For I know the plans I have you," declares the Lord, "plans to prosper you and not to harm you, plans to give you a future and a hope."

Trust Him.

Enough said.

. . .

10

Psalms 6:3 (NIV) "My soul is in anguish. How long, O Lord, how long?"

Must I wait in this restroom line?

Do you know how many "how longs" there are in the book of Psalms? Neither do I - but there are a lot. David seemed to always be crying out to God for an answer to the universal question – "How long, oh Lord?" Is it just me? Or does this speak to you about how impatient God's people are?

Now granted, waiting can be torturous especially if you are pregnant, a week and a half overdue, and dilated to only a half a centimeter (been there). Or if your two-year-old daughter has dislocated her elbow, is crying out in pain, and you are in a packed ER waiting room with several people in line ahead of you (done that).

Now I know these are exaggerated circumstances, but what if you are simply in a long line at the grocery store? To make matters worse, there is melting ice cream in your shopping cart and you haven't eaten since breakfast? Or it's seven in the evening and you are waiting for a table at your favorite restaurant?

I hate waiting and yet ironically, I also hate to be late. So, I get there early and have to wait. It's a personal conundrum.

My husband Greg dislikes sitting through the previews and advertisements that are before all movies. I would rather watch popcorn dancing with a hotdog then stumble into the dark theater right before the movie starts and knock someone's *Jujubes* out of their hands on my way to a seat.

The point is nobody likes to wait. We live in a fast food society where all we have to do is press a button on a remote control to instantly watch our favorite television show. We now can have meals delivered to our door, or even groceries. Instead of waiting for a seat at a restaurant we can order online and pick up dinner on our way home from work. We can even order a movie online and avoid going to the theater at all.

But what if your need is truly great and you are waiting on God for deliverance? What if your child has turned his back on the

Lord and you are left helplessly watching him fall deeper and deeper into sin? What if the tortuous-teen years have stretched to tormenting-twenties or worse, for-the-love-of-God forties?

What if you are dealing with a horrendous debilitating illness and you need a miracle from God now?

David understood this concept. When his enemies were prevailing against him, he wrote these words in Psalms 27:3, "I would have despaired unless I had believed that I would see the goodness of the Lord in the land of the living."

If you are waiting for God to bring your child back to Himself or waiting for a miracle of healing for yourself or someone you love - don't stop believing. Don't stop trusting. Hang onto the horns of the altar, fast, pray, cry out to God.

Allow the knot in your stomach to be a constant reminder to pray without ceasing. Not only will your faith grow during the waiting period, but you will see the goodness of the Lord in the land of living. I, like David, can testify to the goodness of the Lord. I have seen His healing hand on my granddaughter. I have seen His mercy and deliverance in my children. And I have seen his provision in restoring my family after losing my first husband.

Psalms 27:14 (NAS) "Wait for the Lord; Be strong, and let your heart take courage; Yes, wait for the Lord."

. . .

11

Romans 5:8 (NIV) "But God demonstrates His own love for us in this: While we were sinners, Christ died for us."

Wait a minute. Does "us" include me?

I am the baby of the family and because of that title I have never received the respect I deserve as a human being. It's true. In fact, all first-borns reading this book (except for my sweet sister who loves me to death) are probably looking upon that confession saying to themselves, "She's the baby of the family? She has nothing relevant to say. Why am I reading this book?"

Fine. Go ahead. Give the book to your little sister – she'll love it!

I have two sisters who are six, and nine years older than me. They were out gallivanting at malt shops while I was struggling to learn the English language. (Yes, I'm an American citizen and yes there used to be malt shops).

During my teenage years, my sisters were gone, and I was like an only child. Then when my first-born sister and her two children came to live with us for a season, I became a first-born/middle-child. So, to sum it up, I am actually a baby-first-born-middle-child. Basically, I'm a mixed-up mess. So, if you give any credence to the first-born, middle-child, baby scenario, you will now understand why it's amazing that I am even able to write a book let alone have anything relevant to say.

But God in His mercy chose me to be His own. Why? I have no idea. I was bought with a price. He loves me as I am. I can't possibly measure up to His goodness. There is no way on earth I can earn my way to heaven. I will never be able to repay Him for His sacrifice on the cross. All I can possibly do is keep moving forward, fall down, get back up, ask for forgiveness, and continue to offer myself as a sacrifice to the only One who can do anything relevant with my life.

His love is my mission in life. His Word is my guide. There is no way I could have walked through the death of my first husband without God in my life. If you don't believe me, ask my closest friends. There is no way I could have walked through the anguish of watching one of my children as she struggled with issues in her life that were too big for me to handle if I didn't cling to the One and only true living God.

I am not perfect. You may witness me doing or saying something that I shouldn't have done or said. Welcome to reality. This is why I need Jesus. This is why I need His sacrifice on the cross.

This is why you need Him too.

. . .

12

Psalms 141:3 (NAS) "Set a guard, O Lord, over my mouth; keep watch over the door of my lips."

A guard? I need a muzzle!

Why is it, I wonder, that a simple trip to the grocery store can render a normally mellow Christian woman into a raving lunatic? I can be driving along, minding my own business, even lost in a worship song on the radio when suddenly someone pulls out in front of me and then goes ten miles an hour under the speed limit. As I slam on my brakes, I can feel my jaw tightening, my nostrils flaring, and then before I know it, I have thrown all self-control out the window with words like, "You, idiot!" or "You, moron!" (Or worse)

Now granted the window is actually closed (hey, I don't want to get shot) and the driver can't hear me, but it is what has happened within me that is a concern. Why do I react with such hostility to bothersome inconveniences? Where does this anger and frustration come from?

The Bible says, in Matthew 12:34b (KJV) "...For out of the abundance of the heart the mouth speaketh." If these are the things that come out of my mouth, my heart is in big trouble.

Can anyone out there relate to this scenario? Or have you upon reading this thrown yourself onto the floor to begin intercession on my behalf? (If so, thank you!)

Now I know I'm not the only one with these kinds of issues. You may say, "My husband reacts like this, but not me. I'm as pure as the driven snow." Well, even snow drifts on occasion and since none of us are perfect there may be other inconveniences that ruffle your feathers and cause your self-control to fly out the window.

Perhaps, the way your husband chews ice cubes (chomp, chomp, crunch, crunch...). Maybe it's the way the children ignore you when you tell them to pick up their clothes or wipe their feet before entering the house. It could be an issue with a neighbor, a sister, a parent, co-worker that sets you on your last nerve and causes things to flow from your mouth that you know are not sanctified by the Holy Spirit. Or maybe it is simply the *tone* of your voice that does not reflect the love you have for your family.

Thanks be to God for His mercy, forgiveness, and patience! Thank the Lord for the blood of Jesus that washes away our guilt and sin! I am so grateful for my Lord and Savior who walks with me daily, gently nudges me to repentance, and encourages me to keep focused on Him so that one day, one fine day the words of my mouth will only reflect the joy and peace He has placed in my heart.

Until then, does anyone know where I can get a muzzle – size medium?

. . .

13

Matthew 22:39b (NAS) "You shall love your neighbor as yourself."

"Houston, we have a problem!"

I don't like myself much. Never have. For one thing I am only five feet, two and a half inches tall and wear a size nine shoe. I look like an "L". Then to add insult to injury, I have flat feet AND cankles, (you know, those ankles that extend straight down from the calf). I mean really, Lord, what were you thinking?

I have weird ears, too, like no one else in my family. My hair gets frizzy at the suggestion of humidity and it is quite possible that in a tight squeeze I could use my bulbous nose for a flotation device. Any other Germans out there who can relate to this scenario?

In all seriousness though, this concerns me. If I don't love myself, then how can I love others?

We all have things we don't like about ourselves. This is human nature. There is not a perfect person on this planet – even supermodels need airbrushing in order to grace magazine covers. I may not be thrilled with the way my hair looks at the beach and I may never be able to wear stilettos on these feet, but this is not what love of self is all about.

If I'm thirsty, I give myself a drink. If I'm hungry, I feed myself. When I broke my left cankle by falling down the stairs, I wrapped it, hopped on one foot to my car, and drove myself to Urgent Care. Now, if that isn't love, I don't know what is!

God's command in this scripture is for us to simply show the same love to others.

I once noticed an elderly woman standing at the top of a mall escalator with a distraught expression on her face. I never saw the woman before, and I wasn't even a hundred percent sure why she was standing there. But I took a chance, walked up to her, and asked her if she needed my arm to hang onto on the way down. She accepted my help with gratitude. It only took a couple minutes of my time and was a simple gesture that I believe showed God's love to someone in need.

Did I love myself at the time? Well, I wasn't exactly crazy about the body I had been trying to stuff into a bathing suit before the encounter, but I definitely fed that same body lunch that day!

If we are to understand this passage of scripture, we need to read a little more of the chapter.

Matthew 22:36-39 (NAS) "Teacher, which is the great commandment in the Law? And He said to him, you shall love the Lord your God with all your heart, and with all your soul, and with all your mind. This is the great and foremost commandment. And a second is like it, you shall love your neighbor as yourself."

If we truly love the Lord with all our heart, soul, and mind, then showing the love of Jesus to others should really be a piece of cake.

. . .

14

Luke 6:31(NIV) "Do to others as you would have them do to you."

Come on! It's that simple?

I used to work at the front desk of a government-funded rental assistance program. During my first week of employment, a tall red-headed woman with fire in her eyes and the tongue of a serpent entered the lobby. Okay, she was simply disgruntled, but you get the picture. As she waited in line, she was loudly bad-mouthing the program to other people and spewing all forms of hatred towards anyone who would listen. I have to admit, I was a little nervous as she approached.

When it was finally her turn, she was none too thrilled to see a new person at the window. In fact, this seemed to make her even more agitated. So, I did my best to greet her with a smile and offer my assistance, which, I might add, had zero effect in calming her down.

Now, being it was the first week of this particular job, my inclination was to grab my purse, drag my chin out the door, and immediately look for new employment. But instead I made a vow that day to win her over. Over time, not only did she begin greeting me with the same courtesy I extended to her, but we actually developed a bit of a bond. In fact, when I left the job, she told me (in no uncertain terms) that she hated to see me go.

Was this easy to do? No way. I am not personally fond of verbal abuse, and like the next guy, my first choice is fight-or-flight. But I simply decided that day to be different - to do what did not come naturally to me.

"Do to others as you would have them do to you."

Most people have heard this before and don't even know that it is a verse from the Bible. It may even grace their coffee mug at work or a bumper sticker on the rear of their vehicle, and yet they don't have a clue that this was a command spoken from the mouth of Jesus.

To the world it is known as the "Golden Rule." However, unlike gold which rises and falls in value, its value never wavers. There is so much wisdom contained in this single sentence, it boggles the mind. Well, at least it boggles my mind.

If I don't like people to be sarcastic to me (it really chaps my hide) then I shouldn't be sarcastic to them. Simple, right? But what if they ARE sarcastic to me pretty much on a daily basis? Does this give me the right to return a zinger to them in retaliation?

What if a guy cuts me off in traffic? Should I get in the next lane, speed up, and cut him off as well? I mean, he deserves it, right? He needs to be taught a lesson! Unfortunately, this dangerous stunt seems to feed the ego for a brief moment, but it does not in any way please God.

Jesus isn't saying here that we should treat others how we want to be treated ONLY if they treat us nice first. Good heavens! That would be way too easy!! God is always looking at our heart, desiring for us to grow, teaching us to be like Him.

Before His crucifixion, when the soldiers were beating Jesus, did He retaliate by rendering them senseless with a series of brilliant Chuck Norris-style Karate moves? No. Could He have? Of course! When they spit on Him and called Him names, did He spit right back and call them what they actually were? No. He had every right to.

Instead, Jesus forgave them. Then He did something so kind, so loving, so amazingly self-sacrificing that no one else could ever come close to returning the favor. He willingly allowed Himself to be nailed to a cross and crucified for the sake of all mankind.

If that doesn't boggle the mind, I don't know what does.

. . .

15

Psalms 42:11 (NASV) "Why are you in despair, O my soul? And why have you become disturbed within me? Hope in God, for I shall yet praise Him, the help of my countenance and my God."

Don't mind me. I'm just talking to myself.

I have a confession to make. You may want to sit down for this. Oh, you're already sitting down. Yes, it's rather uncomfortable to stand up and read a book - gotcha. Well then, at least brace yourself, because what I'm about to tell you may shock you to the bone.

I'm not always happy.

Gasp! Sputter! What??!! But you were only cracking jokes a moment ago. You have Jesus in your heart, you are redeemed and sanctified by His death on the cross, and you have a home awaiting you in heaven! How can you not be happy?

Makes no sense to me either.

But sometimes (especially now since I have entered the wonderful years of menopause), I feel a sense of heaviness, a deep sadness, and even at times despair. It is like a dark cloud forms above my head and the weight of the world makes its home on my shoulders. Why is that?

Could it be that my spirit longs for its heavenly home? Could it be that the things of this earth are growing "strangely dim?"

I didn't want to write about this. I didn't. It is so difficult to relive the death of my first husband that every time I do, I fall apart. But quite frankly, there is no other way to say it, so here goes.

Yes, it happened a long time ago. Yes, I am now married to another wonderful man. And yes, God has restored my life in so many ways that I am humbled beyond belief. But I have to say that the day I lost Jack took a chunk out of my heart that can only be replaced by heaven.

The moment the doctor led me into the brightly-lit hospital room where Jack's body lay on a cold metal table covered only by a thin white sheet and I looked at his face drained of color, vacant of all that was truly him, I had to ask myself this question: Where was he? Where was my wonderful loving husband? Where was my daughters' doting playful father? To where did the smile lines around his eyes disappear? Where were the dry jokes for which he was so known? Where was the zest for life that daily inspired me to be a better woman? Then I knew. He was no longer there but had passed on from his temporary shell to the eternal.

At that moment heaven became so real to me - so utterly tangible that I felt as if I could have reached up and touched it. And ever since that day when I am feeling low, a deep longing wells up within me, and I yearn for my own heavenly home.

It's not uncommon for Christians to feel sad. Life can be so hard. Pardon my vernacular - but this ain't heaven! If we truly grasp the hope set before us - the knowledge that one day this life will pass, and we will all be home with our Father God - we will make it through.

So, until that day arrives, when despair and sadness try to overtake me, I will remember that this temporal life is simply a step to the eternal, that there is a place prepared for me in heaven, and one day soon, I know not when, I will meet my reward upon His throne and face-to-face I shall praise Him, the help of my countenance and my God.

I wrote this poem to myself shortly after losing my husband:

Oh, heart, how selfishly you crave the one
gone before you to the grave,
Whose most precious years you were blessed
to share
Yet the pain so difficult to bear would still
call him from heaven's gates so fair.
Oh, heart, how selfishly you see. Wanting
only what's good for thee.
Would you call him from the place where he
sees Christ face-to-face?
Tis' the home you, too, long to embrace.
Mary Beth (Stevens) Roosa 1986

. . .

16

2 Corinthians 4:16 (NAS) "Therefore we do not lose heart, but though our outer man is decaying, yet our inner man is being renewed day by day.

Decaying? So THAT'S what's happening here!

I'm going to be blunt. Growing old sucks. I know. I shouldn't use the word "sucks" because it really isn't proper. But I can find no other modern term that clearly expresses my feelings about the physical aging process.

For one thing, it can be embarrassing. Like the time I took a yoga class with my daughter. While music played softly in the background and everyone else in the room was bent serenely in the downward dog position, I was hopping around my mat trying to get rid of a Charlie horse in my calf. Mind you, this is the same woman who used to do backbends in the family room and fold her legs easily into the Lotus position (not at the same time, of course).

Here are a few of the grievances I have regarding growing old:

1) Less hair on my head – more on my face.
2) Upper arms like a flying squirrel - I could probably get lift-off in a hurricane.
3) Ordering off the senior menu without anyone asking me for I.D. (Of all the nerve!)
4) Everything on my body heading south – I figure by the time I'm 80, I'll be in Argentina.
5) Insomnia – this may be partially due to an addiction to *Words with Friends*, or perhaps the disturbance of the snoring pillow next to me – nevertheless, it is annoying.
6) Forgetfulness - I could certainly go on and on with the list, but I forgot what I was going to say.

I mean, seriously, wasn't it yesterday that I was in grade school ducking under my desk when bomb sirens rang out? Was it really that long ago that I was playing British

Bulldog with a bunch of neighborhood kids in the neighbor's front yard until my dad would whistle for me to come home?

Where did the time go? My husband, Greg, and I have often talked about how when we were still in school it seemed like an eternity until we graduated. But after graduation, we blinked and suddenly, we were more than a half a century old.

As precious as the memories are to me, I don't want to relive my childhood. No, thank you! But why can't I at least have the same energy and vitality that I had when I was young?

When I was a teenager, I may not have had to stretch my muscles before hopping out of bed in the morning in order to not fall flat on my face, but I also had zero wisdom. (If you knew some of the guys I dated, you would earnestly agree.) But as I grew in my walk with the Lord and began studying His scriptures, my life began to change.

James 1:6 (NAS) "But if any of you lack wisdom let him ask of God who gives to all men generously and without reproach and it will be given to him."

Knowledge of God's Word is vital to the Christian life. Everything we need can be found in His Word. But to me, the wisdom to utilize that knowledge is a priceless jewel God offers freely and can change our lives like nothing else.

And so, as my skin continues its fight with gravity and my energy slips slowly away, I will rejoice in the God who renews my inner-self day by day and continue to pray for the wisdom to live my life, whatever it has in store for me, to the fullest.

. . .

17

Proverbs 27:17 (NAS) "Iron sharpens iron,
so one man sharpens another."

That's gotta hurt!

My husband Greg and I are polar opposites in so many ways. Besides the obvious man/woman differences, we come from entirely different backgrounds and completely different ways of thinking. It has definitely caused some major friction in our marriage.

I'm a minimalist. He is a collector. I am a planner. He loves spontaneity. We are both frugal, but I love, love, love to give. Greg can squeeze a penny so tightly that I've seen Lincoln's eyeballs pop out of his head, and he is always looking for new ways to save money.

For instance, he once heard a lady on a talk show say that if you put a dry towel in the dryer with your wet clothes the clothes will dry faster. I'm not sure if it works or not, but every load of laundry I remove from the dryer now includes a towel. This used to irritate the life out of me. I mean, seriously, I have done laundry for over forty years – how dare someone try to change the way I do things without asking me first!

Our conflicting ways of thinking became evident early in our marriage when I pointed to a house and said, "nice bricks." He replied back, "nice blocks," and then spent the next ten minutes explaining to me the difference between a brick and a block. To this day "brick-block" has become our go-to phrase when we don't agree on something.

Me: Did you lock the Arcadia door?
Greg: Yes, I locked the *patio* door.
Me: Brick-block.

Sometimes our differences are not so funny, and this is where the sharpening comes in. Like most married couples, we have had our share of ugly encounters. In fact, right before writing this chapter we had a doozy! (Ironic – isn't it?) It was so bad that I actually considered throwing in the towel – but then I knew he'd just toss it back into the dryer!

WIGGLING ON THE ALTAR

Whether married or not, God uses relationships to work out areas in our lives that aren't pleasing to Him. It's not fun, and it can be downright painful. But, if we remember that it's not our job to change the other person, (only God can perform miracles), then we can focus on the areas of our lives that need change. Now this isn't something that is easy to do – especially when we are angry or wounded. But if we remember why we must go through conflicts, it will be worth it when we are on the other side of them.

James 1:2-4 (NAS) "Consider it all joy my brethren, when you encounter various trials, knowing that the testing of your faith produces endurance. And let endurance have its perfect result, that you may be perfect and complete, lacking in nothing."

I personally have not reached the level of considering it "all joy" when my loved one and I butt heads. But I am thankful that I have a God who walks me through the battles of life, causes me to grow through them, and is preparing a place for me in heaven. Quite frankly, it doesn't matter to me if my heavenly mansion is made of bricks or blocks, because I will finally be home.

. . .

18

2 Corinthians 6:14 (NIV) "Do not be yoked together with unbelievers. For what do righteousness and wickedness have in common? Or what fellowship can light have with darkness?"

Does this mean that those sharing this yoke will always work together like a synchronized swim team? Ya? No.

Raising teenagers is not for the faint of heart. They go from birth - when they need you twenty-four hours a day - to teenagers not really wanting to be seen with you in public. It's like they don't want their friends to know they have a mother. I mean – ew!

I had the privilege (and near nervous breakdown) of raising six teenage daughters, (and a teenage son who incidentally gave me zero problems). Can you even comprehend the amount of money we spent on feminine products??

Nevertheless, God gave me daughters so that:

1) I could instill in their lives everything God has taught me about Him.
2) Retribution for the grief I gave my own mother.

I grew up in the 60s and 70s without trying drugs. As I look back, I realize what a miracle that was considering most of my peers smoked a little wacky-tobacky and I had easy access to pretty much any drug I could have wanted. To help you understand how rare this phenomenon was, later on in life when I was taking a polygraph test for the eligibility of volunteering at the police department, this question came up. When I told the interviewer that, "No, I never did drugs," he stopped, peered over his glasses at me, and replied, "even I smoked marijuana!"

What can I say? I was a Jesus freak. There is actually a picture in one of my yearbooks of me walking to class with my Bible clutched tightly in my arms. This testimony, however, did not always keep me from certain compromising situations. Let me tell you, even a teen on fire for the Lord has the opportunity to fall into temptation. This is why the moment my daughters entered their teenage years, I cried out, often and loudly, to God Almighty on their behalf and asked for wisdom on how to keep them from evil.

There were many things I wanted to instill in my children as they grew, some of which were: a deep and passionate love for the Lord, loyalty to family and friends, a servant's heart, and a giving spirit. But one thing that lay heavy on my heart was whom they would eventually marry. (I mean this dude was going to end up my son-in-law, hello!)

I prayed often that God would give my children wisdom and discernment in their relationships and prayed for divine intervention regarding how, when, and even where they would meet. From my viewpoint, meeting a future spouse in a sleazy bar or nightclub is like washing your car in a haboob or taking a bath in a mud puddle – the outcome will be less than satisfactory.

But how was I to instill these convictions into the hearts of my children?

When shoving the scripture about being equally yoked down their throats at least once a week didn't produce great results, I began crying out to God for something I could say that would be easier for them to swallow and would stick with them as they encountered the dating scene.

This is what the Lord gave me, and quite frankly, I think it was brilliant: "Don't settle for Ishmael, when Isaac is on his way."

After God promised Abraham and Sarah a son, they had to wait a long, long time before His promise was fulfilled – we are talking way past receiving their first Social Security check. Sarah, seeing her biological clock ticking away decided to "assist" God by encouraging her husband to have relations with her servant (talk about desperation!). That is how Ishmael came to be. He was Abraham's son. But he was not the son God had promised. He was man's choice. He was not God's choice.

My daughters, like most young women their age, experienced some Ishmaels before meeting their Isaacs. Some of their relationships caused them deep heartbreak, were heart wrenching to watch, and sent me flying to my knees on more than one occasion. As their mother, all I could do was to stand on the faith that God had their best interest in mind, that He would be faithful to bring about the men He desired for them in

His timing. I never stopped praying until my youngest daughter met the man of her dreams.

All of my kids are now married, and LOVE, LOVE, LOVE all of their spouses. What a blessing! What a miracle! Even now I have tears in my eyes as I consider God's goodness as He answered the cries of a mother's heart. He didn't have to. I am nobody special. All I did was lay my children down at His feet and let God do His thing.

One more point I feel necessary to add. Does being equally yoked keep your children from struggling in their relationships? Do they ever have disagreements or even bitter arguments with their spouses? Of course, they do. I did not give birth to robots.

We are all human. We all need Jesus. Just like my husband and I, our children have to work on their marriages to keep it fresh. They have to choose love and forgiveness even when it is difficult to do so. And they have to daily put on the only yoke they will ever truly need.

Matthew 11:29-30 (NAS) "Take My yoke upon you, and learn from Me, for I am gentle and humble in heart, and you shall find rest for your souls. For My yoke is easy, and my load is light."

19

2 Timothy 1:7 (NKJ) "For God has not given us a spirit of fear, but of power and of love and of a sound mind."

It is quite possible He is still working on the "sound mind" part.

I was born an introvert. I can still remember as a young child hiding behind my mother's dress at church, too shy to shake the pastor's hand. I can also remember quite clearly how I sobbed like a baby the first day of school when my mother peeled me off of her leg and walked out of the classroom.

I'm not a leader. I'm a follower. I would rather write a book in the privacy of my office than speak in public. Some get recharged by being around large groups of people; I get recharged by being alone.

My friends would probably say, "That's preposterous! She is not shy! Give that girl a cappuccino, and she'll talk your ear off!"

WIGGLING ON THE ALTAR

This is true. When caffeine hits my blood stream, it is like truth serum. However, it took me years to step out of my inhibitions and I couldn't have done it without one particular friend.

I met Kathy when we were both three-years-old. Right after we moved into her neighborhood, her mother marched her across the street, and we became instant friends. Kathy, also the baby of the family, is not an introvert. Kathy is an extrovert. I can only describe Kathy as a woman who walks into the room mouth first, and I say that with the utmost respect. Kathy and her mouth are the reason my life changed dramatically at the age of 15.

Kathy went to a Pentecostal church. I went to a Lutheran church. As far back as I can remember Kathy was in revival. One time when she spent the night (we were probably 9 years old), we got into an argument over something stupid. In the darkness of my bedroom I could see her arms lifted toward the ceiling.

Me: What are you doing?
Kathy: Praying.
Me: Put your arms down.
Kathy: No.

Me: Put your arms down or get out of my bed.

Without a word, Kathy got out of bed and sat in a rocking chair across the room from me. By the moonlight peering in through a break in the curtains, I could see her rocking back and forth, back and forth, her arms fully extended to the heavens.

I had a lot of fears as a child. I wouldn't do anything unless Kathy did it first. I took a speech class in High School because she was in my class. I took drama in High School only because she dragged me with her. And one time at a carnival, I made her go on the Round Up three times before I got up enough nerve to go on it with her.

As we hit puberty, a gap began to grow in our relationship. As a Lutheran, I believed that Jesus was my Savior. I knew He was the only way to heaven. Yet, even though we went to church every time the church doors opened, there were a lot of gray areas in my life.

Kathy began to tell me about miracles she had witnessed at her church and testimonies of missionaries who saw God do great things – things I had never heard before in the Lutheran church. Because of her enthusiasm regarding the things of God, a hunger began to slowly develop within me. I began to desire something deeper, something more in my relationship with God. Because of Kathy's persistence in wanting me to come with her to church, I finally gave in. It was that night that I had an encounter with the Holy Spirit that would change my relationship with God forever.

1 John 4:18a (NKJ) "There is no fear in love; but perfect love casts out fear…"

Because God loved me so much, He sent me a friend who was not afraid to tell me everything she knew about Him. Am I still an introvert? Well, you are not going to get me on the Round Up anytime soon or hear me preaching the Gospel from my rooftop. In fact, if the Lord ever called me to preach, I'd probably be like Jonah and take a long walk off a short whale. But if you want to know why I love Jesus, go ahead, keep reading.

. . .

20

Matthew 7:7a (NAS) "Ask, and it shall be given to you; seek, and you shall find; knock, and it shall be opened for you."

Ok. I would like some chocolate, please.

As I mentioned before, I have a huge family. And consequently, the more people in a household, the more items get lost. No matter how organized I tried to be, it was inevitable that at some point something significant was misplaced at the exact moment someone needed it – like car keys, tools, books, clothing, or cell phones.

This happened more frequently to one particular member of the family whose name will be changed to protect the innocent. Let's call this person I. M. Frantic.

It used to frustrate the life out of me watching Frantic run around the house, rifling through piles, tossing things in the air, and grumbling because they couldn't find something they desperately needed. And it wasn't that I didn't understand their dilemma. I did. When I am rushed, discombobulated, and looking for something that I need right at that very moment, my brain shuts off. And without a brain, it's difficult to think. (You can quote me on that).

Then one day I got a revelation. Hello! Why don't I ask the Lord for help? I mean, He may not be that concerned about a missing sock or a lost jacket, but I know He is concerned about the person looking for it. So, I asked Frantic to stop searching for a moment, leave the area, and let me have a shot at it.

And after they left the room, I took a deep breath to calm my spirit (it's amazing how contagious frustration can be), and then took a moment to stop, pray, and ask God to direct me to missing item. I mean, God *was* the only one who knew where it was, right? Within moments - and I'm not exaggerating - I walked right into a room and found the missing item! Let me tell you, I was more shocked than anyone. It's funny how we can believe God for something and when He accomplishes it, we can't believe it.

So, this has been my system now for years and it always works. Do I always find the item right away? No. Sometimes it has taken a day or two. But the answer is in the asking, the seeking, and the knocking. When we are sensitive to the prompting of the Holy Spirit, we can move in faith with the confidence that God wants to be included in every area of our lives no matter how insignificant we may think it is.

Over the years this has happened to me countless times. I'm not sure how coworkers found out about it, but even they began asking me to help them find things. And every time I prayed, God always came through for them, and it became a great testimony to my friends of God's love for them!

Do I have some special gift? No. Do I possess some sort of super-power? Nope, (which is good because I look like the Michelin Man in leotards). I have simply learned that as we walk with God through even the daily mundane things of life, He will never fail us. He wants to be with us and included in everything we do. If He didn't, He would have never said these words:

Hebrews 13:5b (NKJ) "…I will never leave you nor forsake you."

21

Proverbs 17:22 (NAS) "A joyful heart is good medicine, but a broken spirit dries up the bones."

If you ask me, there are an awful lot of dried up bones out there!

What is wrong with the human race these days? I mean, I pride myself in being a nice person, sometimes perhaps overly so, but nevertheless I try to greet friends and strangers alike with at least a smile or hello whenever possible. Now keep in mind, I was born an introvert, so it has taken years for me to come out of my shell and even look another human being in the face.

My mother was the friendliest person on the planet. She worked as a receptionist at our local doctor's office and more than once I watched her greet patients with the same respect and courtesy, she did members of our church. I have vivid memories of women standing in line behind her, waiting for a chance to talk to her after a Sunday service. People loved my mother! Her genuine warmth and natural kindness simply made people want to be around her. And because of that I have spent years working to emulate her.

However, not everyone on this planet is friendly. And if you can believe it, not everyone has a sense of humor.

I know, crazy, huh?

My trip to the grocery store this morning proved that fact. Now, granted, grocery shopping doesn't always generate a good mood, and I get that. We've all had moments where we simply wanted to rush into the store, grab what we need off the shelf, and hurry out to our car without interruption. But how difficult is it to return a smile as you pass someone in the aisle? I mean, all you have to do is encourage the corners of your lips to reach for your nostrils and there you have it – a grin!

Unfortunately, on this particular day as I was cruising up and down the aisles, blessing strangers with a glimpse of my newly bleached teeth, I was either dismissed as if I was yesterday's iPhone or glared at like I was an escapee from planet *Xandor*.

Not even ONE person smiled back. I mean, come on! This is Mesa, Arizona - not Hollywood, California (aka - the BOTOX capital of the world)!

This bothered me so much that after I packed the grocery bags into my car and slithered into the driver's seat, I examined my reflection in the mirror to make sure there was nothing disturbing stuck between my teeth or strange hanging from my face (besides my nose). When nothing was awry, I let out a heavy sigh, thrust the key in the ignition, and started the car.

As I was about to back out of the parking space and head home, it happened. A man, probably in his early thirties, ushering his young son out of the vehicle next to me, not only graced me with a smile as I waited for him to pass safely behind my vehicle, but waved at me as well.

This solitary man, this stranger who had no clue of my current discouragement, brightened my entire morning with a single grin.

We have no idea what goes on in the lives of those we pass on a daily basis. Perhaps they are discouraged, sad, or frustrated. Perhaps, they are simply rushed and tired. They could be grieving a lost loved one or having a difficult time making ends meet. Life isn't easy, and it is much more comfortable to allow the muscles in our face to sag downward as we rush past people, than to make the effort to grace them with genuine warmth.

But what if I smile at them and they don't return the gesture? (Welcome to my world!) At least we know we did our part to shine the love of Jesus in their direction. And who knows, perhaps that single joyful gesture may work like medicine on their weary heart, brighten their morning as well, and open the door for us to share with them the true reason we are smiling.

. . .

22

Mark 11:25-26 (NKJV) "And whenever you stand praying, if you have anything against anyone, forgive him, that your Father in heaven may also forgive you your trespasses. But if you do not forgive, neither will your Father in heaven forgive your trespasses."

Ouch!

Wife: Will you forgive me?
Husband: Why? What did you do?
Wife: First, I need to know if you will forgive me.
Husband: Is this a trick question?

God's command for us to forgive is straightforward. In order to be forgiven, we need to forgive others. Nowhere in scripture does God give us the option of waiting to forgive those who offend us until we "feel" like it.

I don't know about you, but when

someone hurts me - says or does something that seriously wounds me - my first response is not sunshine and lollipops. Quite frankly, I either want to remove myself as far from them as possible or smack them upside the head. But since removing oneself far from them would require expensive airline tickets to Mozambique or Madagascar, and striking them could result in prison time, I figure it is much easier to be obedient to God first and allow my feelings to follow.

We are all human and being that we are human we are going to hurt one another. It's a fact. It's not pretty, but it's a fact. We can spend our lives reliving those hurts repeatedly and allowing bitterness to squeeze off the flow of God's love to our hearts, or we can release them to God and be obedient to His word.

Forgiveness is simply an act, not an emotion. The words "I forgive you" have healing written all over them. Once out of your mouth, you will be amazed at the change that takes place in your heart. It may not happen instantly, but trust me, it will happen.

Also, forgiveness works both ways. Not only must we forgive, but we must also ask for forgiveness when the fault is ours.

WIGGLING ON THE ALTAR

When I was still single, I spent many late nights alone in my bedroom reading the Word, praying, and seeking God about a future spouse. My focus was for God to prepare me, so I was everything I needed to be as a wife and mother.

Now believe me, I am not bragging here. On the contrary, I was clinging by my teeth to the horns of the altar, terrified that if God didn't do something with the mess I had already made of my life, that one sight of me and my faults would cause the man of my dreams to run like the wind.

Let me warn you - God loves prayers for change! No sooner had I uttered a request for improvement in my life that the Lord reminded me of someone from my past to whom I needed to ask forgiveness. Yikes!

I could have easily reminded the Lord that this person was also a Christian and was as guilty as I was, but I knew in my heart that it wasn't my business how God dealt with them. It was about changing me.

After inquiring about the person's whereabouts from a mutual friend, I was suddenly off the hook! The person had moved out-of-state, and my friend did not have their phone number or address. Woo-hoo! Maybe I hadn't really heard from God after all, and I was free from the extremely uncomfortable conversation I had so nervously anticipated.

Wrong.

The very next Sunday morning, no sooner had I entered the sanctuary of the church I had been attending, that I heard my name being called from across the long foyer. You got it. That person to whom I was to confront had moved back to Arizona that very weekend. What were the odds?

God had required something of me, and then He prepared the way for me to achieve it. Even though the other person was hesitant in forgiving me (most likely because that would be an admission of their guilt as well), being obedient to God released me from guilt and allowed me to walk into my future with a clean slate. What an amazing feeling that was!

Forgiveness is a daily process. We sin - we ask God to forgive us. We blow it with a family member or friend - we ask for their forgiveness. They hurt us, whether knowingly or not - we must forgive them and then allow God to take care of the wounds.

I want nothing to separate me from my relationship with God. If that means I must be the one who humbles myself first, then so be it! Is it ever easy? No way. Do I sometimes allow my emotions to take over the situation? You betcha'!

I once heard a pastor say these words: "The one with the most faith is the one who forgives first." I love that! Can you imagine how much better this world would be, if we as Christians would begin to apply this simple admonition to our everyday lives?

. . .

23

Philippians 4:6 (NAS) "Be anxious for nothing, but in everything by prayer and supplication with thanksgiving let your requests be made known to God."

This is much harder than it looks – at least for me.

For some strange reason after your age rolls over into the "sixties category," doctors suddenly recommend you undergo every test in their medical book. It appears to me that they are determined to shake everything that's loose (and I'm not talking about the skin under my arms). Perhaps physicians assume if they shake hard enough or burrow deep enough that they are liable to find something amiss.

Hello!

There I was minding my own business having a few mild and only slightly annoying heart palpitations (same kind as I've had my entire life, mind you) when a couple of my daughters ordered me to make an appointment. Well, since the doctor I hadn't seen for over three years was now retired, I made an appointment to see the new M.D. who took his place.

Going to the doctor is stressful enough, but having to go to a brand new doctor produced enough anxiety in me that it raised my blood pressure from low to medium-high (to which I instantly blamed on menopause, caffeine, and the fact that I had to go to the doctor).

After being poked and prodded by cold calloused hands (and that was just to get me on the scale), I had blood drawn and an EKG, which thankfully turned out normal. Even my cholesterol was under the recommended limit. Not bad for a diet that included all forms of cheese, toffee-covered peanuts, ice cream, and caffeine. Why then did the doctor encourage me to go see a cardiologist?

I guess, in all honesty I could have avoided the stress of seeing another new doctor by simply not making the appointment. But since the M.D. recommended I go to make sure that the heart palpitations were not a sign of something hidden, and since my insurance card that I spent big bucks on in monthly premiums had been collecting dust in my drawer, I went ahead and took the plunge.

This is when the real anxiety began. For one thing, I was well aware that there was a history of heart problems in my family. I was several pounds overweight. And there were those life-long heart palpitations that all the other doctors had dismissed as normal.

What if all along I had a congenital heart condition that was never addressed? What if I had palpitations during the echocardiogram, and they had to rush me to the hospital for triple bypass surgery? Or worse, what if my shoestring got caught in the treadmill and I fell flat on my face in front of everybody? All these things were building up inside of me as I drove toward the cardiologist office and the unknown.

Of course, I was praying my brains out. Prayers of faith that went something like this:

"I'm too young to die!"

"As much as I can't wait to be with you in heaven, Lord, I haven't finished my book!"

"Lord, don't let me fall off the tread-mill!"

And then I thanked Him for always being with me, no matter what the outcome. As I was beginning to feel the peace of the Lord flood over me and the tension leave my body, my low-inflated-tire signal lit up my dash like a Christmas tree. Welcome to my life.

Well, to make a long story short, I made it to the doctor in time and after enduring two more appointments, I was sent home with a clean bill of health. What about the heart palpitations? The cardiologist said they were probably due to stress.

Hello!

. . .

24

John 3:17 (KJV) "For God sent not his Son into the world to condemn the world; but that the world through him might be saved."

This scripture should cause legalistic Christians everywhere to shake in their boots.

One night I was standing outside a restaurant waiting for friends to arrive when apparently pacing back and forth and continually checking my cell phone made me appear suspicious. After spending a few moments swatting at a moth that felt the need to flutter around my head, a hostess, perhaps judging me as a woman conducting an imaginary orchestra, emerged from the doorway with a concerned look on her face.

"Ma'am," she asked. "Are you all right?"

My first inclination was to respond, "No, are you? Because seriously, are any of us *really* all right?"

WIGGLING ON THE ALTAR

I will be the first to admit I'm far from perfect (my husband will most definitely be the second). In fact, I am probably harder on myself than anyone else in my life. However, constant judgment by others has never had a healthy effect on me, has never helped to improve my life, and because of that I have, unfortunately, had to leave some otherwise precious relationships behind.

Over the years, I have learned to surround myself with friends who love me the way I am, with all my quirks and strange behavior and who do not constantly point out areas of my life that need change. It's not that I refuse to accept criticism from others or do not invite Godly people to speak into my life. I'm talking about not allowing harmful relationships with those who cannot for whatever reason see past my shortcomings.

This world is filled with lives that do not mirror the Word of God. Some sin is hidden, while others feel the need to broadcast their immorality over every form of media for the entire world to see. The fact remains that all of us have sin in our lives, and all of us fall short of the glory of God. Most importantly, all of us deserve God's wrath and judgment.

I love this scripture because it tells us that God did not send Jesus to bring judgment to the world. On the contrary, He sent His Son to bring salvation, love, mercy, and grace. If God, who is the only One with the right to condemn the world, is offering salvation instead of condemnation, what right do we have of casting judgment on others?

Does that mean that when we see sin in the world, we should simply look the other way? On the contrary, God calls us to repent of our own sin and turn away from ungodly behavior. Instead of pointing out the sin in others, why not reach out and allow the grace, mercy, and love that God has poured upon us to draw people to salvation?

My own path to salvation was not paved by judgmental condemning people, but by those who loved me enough to gently point the way. Let us give the world a reason to want Jesus. Be examples of laying down our lives and offering hope. Let us love them to life. Let us be the light that causes them to want to emerge from their own darkness and allow God to do the rest.

. . .

25

James 1:19-20 (NAS) "This you know, my beloved brethren. But let everyone be quick to hear, slow to speak, and slow to anger, for the anger of man does not achieve the righteousness of God."

Yikes!

Have you ever put your foot in your mouth? Not literally, of course. However, if you *can* literally put your foot in your mouth, I must say that is equally impressive as it is unsanitary.

I'm referring to something that has gone forth from your lips that you wish you could grab from the atmosphere and stuff back into your mouth. It could have been something said in a moment of heightened emotion, or perhaps it was a phrase uttered in a public place that was more suggestive than you realized until you saw the color drain from your husband's face.

WIGGLING ON THE ALTAR

Do you ever wish your brain worked faster to stop your lips from flapping? Well, welcome to my entire life!

This is why I'd rather be a writer than a speaker. If I speak the wrong thing I cannot scroll backward and rewrite it. I cannot return to the beginning of the scene and edit. I cannot drag my words to the trashcan icon and delete them. And if the town gossip (yeah, I wrote town gossip) gets a load of it, it's out there for the entire world to hear.

I can repent, I can ask forgiveness, but I can never erase those words from history.

Let's break it down:

1) Quick to hear – Being attentive, a good listener.
2) Slow to speak – If I am a good listener, then I *will* be slow to speak, right?
3) Slow to anger – If I am a good listener *and* slow to speak, then won't that give me more time to consider my response even if what is said stirs up some uncomfortable emotions?

I have a confession to make (yes, another one). I came awfully close to deleting this chapter. I literally almost dragged this sucker to the trash icon and walked away. Because no sooner had I began writing it, when (of course) I responded to something my husband said with a zinger that hit him right between the eyes. I didn't even realize how offensive it was until he quit talking. So, upon revelation (which took a while, because apparently, I'm a little slow), I immediately admitted I was wrong and asked for forgiveness. And thank the Lord he accepted it with grace.

You may ask - what if he said something to you first that set you off? It doesn't matter. My obedience to God is not contingent upon whether or not others offend me – it's contingent upon how I respond. And I'll be the first to admit, it isn't easy.

Some people believe that the Bible is a book of rules too difficult to follow. They are correct. We cannot keep God's commandments without God's help. It is when we realize that the laws of God were placed there for our benefit and protection that it becomes pertinent in our hearts to follow them to the best of our ability and to lean into God's grace, mercy, and forgiveness when we blow it.

. . .

26

Proverbs 15:23 (NAS) "A man has joy in an apt answer. And how delightful is a timely word!"

Synchronize my tongue, oh Lord!

The first time it happened, I was more than hesitant. My entire life I had strolled by these women (and men) without a sideways glance. It wasn't that I felt like I was better than they were. I simply, and foolishly, assumed that since their faces were usually turned downward toward the floor, a sink, (or worse) a toilet that they probably wanted to remain anonymous. I mean, I don't even like cleaning my *own* toilet and couldn't imagine wanting to be acknowledged while slaving over one seat that had been graced (putting it nicely) by a plethora of posteriors.

I was at Phoenix Children's Hospital and was running back and forth from the NICU, where my tiny new granddaughter lay fighting for her life, to a restroom right outside the door. I was standing to the side of the entry, waiting while a middle-aged woman took her time polishing the mirror, scouring the sink, and scrubbing the floors.

At first, I was impatient, wishing she would "put the pedal to the metal," so to speak. I even considered moving down the corridor in search of another facility. When out of the blue it hit me - how incredibly valuable this woman was! Not only had she been doing a job that may not have been her number one career choice, but she was preventing me from transferring germs to the NICU. She probably didn't even realize how profoundly significant that was to the life and health of my precious grandbaby.

Suddenly, overwhelming emotion and gratitude washed over me, and I could feel a sense of urgency to not allow the opportunity to pass me by. As the woman was about to push her cart down the hallway, I stepped in front of her, smiled, and blurted out something like this.

"Hi! I know you probably don't hear this often. But I want you to know that what you do is really important. So, thank you!"

She didn't look at me like I had lost my

marbles. She didn't brush my comment off like it was no big deal. Instead, ever so subtly, like sunshine breaking from behind a cloud, a smile crept slowly across her face. And from that moment on, every time I passed her in the hallway, we smiled at each other and said hello.

I don't know if something was going on in her life at the time or even if she was sick of her job. All I know is that a few simple words spoken with kindness made us both feel good.

I know that I have written a lot about the tongue, but let me tell you, I have a lot of experience in this area - just ask my family (on second thought, please don't). In fact, if I'm being truly honest, the initial M in my name should stand for Mouth. There have been times when it has been my worst enemy, and yet there have been other moments when I found it to be a tool to bless others.

Ephesians 4:29 (NAS) "Let no unwholesome word proceed from your mouth, but only such a word as is good for edification according to the need of the moment, that it may give grace to those who hear."

We have no idea what lies in the hearts

and lives of those we pass by on a daily basis. There will always be those less fortunate, harder working, and more stressed than we could ever imagine. And who knows? A kind word spoken from a sincere heart at the right moment could be like ointment poured upon their wound, a cool drink on a torrid day, or a sliver of sunshine breaking through a storm cloud.

We don't have to wait for an epiphany. We don't need to be suddenly overcome with emotion. In fact, that only happened to me one time. All we need to do is recognize an opportunity and take it.

By the way...you are valuable! You are God's creation and you are loved beyond your wildest dreams.

Just thought you ought to know.

...

27

Psalms 127:3&5a "Sons are a heritage from the Lord, children a reward from him. Blessed is the man whose quiver is full of them."

My quiver is so full, it makes me quiver.

One of my daughters recently asked me this question: "Do you still find blessings from being a mom?" My first response could very well have been: "Define blessings…" But, by the serious look on her face, I knew she was seeking a heartfelt answer rather than a comedy routine using her and her siblings for material.

Truth be told, I am a woman most blessed! My mind cannot even wrap itself around the idea of life without my children. Each time one of them was born, and I looked into their tiny faces for the very first time, it was as if God came down from heaven and handed me His heart. I have learned more about love, faith, and giving by having children than I feel I personally ever could have without.

However, I'm not going to lie. Life with kids hasn't always been rainbows, sunshine, and kittens (which is probably good, since I'm allergic to kittens).

As a parent I have gone through some brutal times.

I experienced seasons with my kids when I felt like I was hanging by my teeth to the edge of the precipice of no return. It was during those times that I discovered a foundation of faith in a God who promised that if I raised my children according to His principles, no matter how far they roamed, they would one day return to the God of their childhood.

And they all did.

There are no perfect parents. Trust me on that! I made every mistake imaginable. You can read every book written on the subject of parenting and the most you will get is confused. We can only walk day by day, moment by moment, seeking God, and trusting that He will not only give us wisdom to raise our unique, one-of-a-kind children, but also that He will clean up any mess we make.

WIGGLING ON THE ALTAR

For those of you for whatever reason do not have children, never fear! You can learn about giving, love, and sacrifice by serving others. The Bible puts it this way:

James 1:27 (NAS) "This is pure and undefiled religion in the sight of our God and Father, to visit orphans and widows in their distress and to keep oneself unstained by the world."

So, in answer to my daughter's question: Yes. Although they are all grown and have their own lives and families, I still find great joy and blessing in being their mom (being a grandma is even better!), and if I had to do it over, I wouldn't change a thing.

You see, I honestly believe that each one of my children and grandchildren are jewels in my crown of life! And, let it be known that one day, when my life on earth is over, I will take that crown of jewels and lay it at the feet of the One and Only true living God – the author and finisher of my faith and the giver of all good things in my life.

. . .

28

Luke 18:27 "What is impossible with men is possible with God."

It doesn't seem possible, does it?

I have no idea why God chose me to be His child. I can't understand why He loves me when most of the time, I don't even like myself. I think about this often lately. If I look back on my life, I see many reasons why God should have never chosen someone like me.

Here are a few examples:

1) I am not hero material - How many flat-footed Bible heroes can you name? Besides that, I tried using a slingshot once and almost took out my own eye!
2) I am not aesthetically beautiful like Sarah or Bathsheba - Take away my blue eyes and what have you got? A squatty body

with a prominent proboscis balancing on two cankles.

3) In spite of my name, I'm more like Martha than Mary – I am worried and bothered about so many things. That reminds me, I forgot to take the laundry out of the dryer, and what on earth am I going to make for supper? Hmmm.

4) I am not genius-material – Paraphrasing a line from Forrest Gump: "I may not be a smart girl. But I do know what love is."

So why would God call someone like me to be His own? Why would He pour His life into someone so undeserving, so (by the world's standards) inadequate? My best answer? He is Love. It is as simple as that.

God is love.

Have you ever experienced a chocolate fountain? Warm, sweet brown heaven pouring down with abandon over and over and all you have to do is willingly reach in with your strawberry or cookie to taste and see that it is good? Granted, this may not be the best example (especially for those allergic to chocolate), but this is how I can envision God's love. It is forever pouring out of Him, and all we have to do is reach in and taste it.

It is so simple it seems impossible. But

what is impossible to man, is possible with God. Once we truly grasp this concept, nothing can stand in our way of reaching for His love, allowing it to flow over us, and then sharing it with others.

...

29

James 4:14 (NAS) "Yet you do not know what your life will be like tomorrow. You are just a vapor that appears for a little while and then vanishes away."

No truer words were ever written.

My life flashed before my eyes.

There were toys I had wanted as a child but never received, like the tiny metal kitchen set or the giant wooden dollhouse. There was a red and white tricycle that I rode until the rubber on one of the back wheels fell off, a metal and vinyl table and chair where I sat every evening as a child eating dinner with my family. I can still hear the chair legs squeaking across the linoleum. There was a toy typewriter with a dial instead of keys that inspired my writing career, gumball machines, Coca-Cola bottles, and the lampshade decorated with a saguaro cactus that sat on wagon wheel side tables in our living room. Even a fancy white bonnet with blue ribbon like I wore one Easter that matched the lacy dress my oldest sister had sewn for me.

No. I did not have a near-death experience.

I walked through an antique store while Patsy Cline's voice flowed from speakers in the ceiling, and I fought back tears. I wondered what to do with the plethora of memories that have gone away with the past.

This life is fleeting. A whirlwind. If you blink, you may miss something. Like I mentioned, my husband and I often talk about how long it seemed to get through our school years. But once out of high school, we were somehow transported in time to an adult community. What? I am eligible for Social Security benefits? How did that happen?

The thought leaves one wondering "what if?" What if I had become a ballerina, like I desired as a child? What if my music aspirations were successful, and I had become a well-known musical sensation? What if instead of being an extra in movies, I was "discovered" and suddenly became rich and famous?

What if all those things had gotten in the

way of the amazing relationship I now have with the Lord?

I wouldn't trade my life walking with Jesus through every valley and mountain top, for all the silver and gold in the world.

. . .

30

Genesis 22:7b (NIV) "The fire and wood are here," Isaac said, "but where is the lamb for the burnt offering?"

What do you mean you're looking at him??!!

My first husband, Jack once told me that if I ever wrote a book, I should title it WIGGLING ON THE ALTAR. He knew how difficult it was for me to let go of certain areas in my life and trust God with the transformation. He witnessed the fear that kept me from releasing my past, present, and future. He held a front row seat as I wrestled with the Holy Spirit over things that I hung onto with my fingers and toes. To prove how accurate he was, in his assessment, it has taken me over thirty years to write this book!

Pitiful, I know.

There isn't much written in Genesis

about Isaac's reaction to being placed on the altar, but I have my suspicions that he did some kicking and screaming as Abraham tied him up. I mean, wouldn't you?

First, Isaac probably felt betrayed by his father. Here they were on a friendly camping trip. Sure, he knew that there would be a sacrifice at some point, but this was father-son bonding time, right? Perhaps, Isaac even felt proud that his father had asked him to join him on this spiritual journey. He had no doubt witnessed Abraham perform the ritual many times and knew that the outcome was death. Can you even imagine the shock and fear that gripped Isaac's heart the moment he realized that *he* was the sacrifice?

Laying down our lives requires pain. It's that simple. Trust me – even writing this book has required pain (and I'm not talking about paper cuts!). I have gone through spiritual warfare. The struggle with my self-worth and doubt of my story's relevance has been so debilitating at times I even considered throwing the unfinished book in the trash.

We were all born into sin. We all have areas in our lives that we would rather others not see. Trust me. Yet, it is only when we are honest about those imperfections and open to examination by the Holy Spirit, that God can do His work in our lives.

Sounds simple, huh? Ya? No.

Well, thankfully, God stopped Abraham's hand from sacrificing Isaac on the altar. I imagine there was an enormous sigh of relief from both father and son, not to mention some hip-hop dancing, fist-pumping, and stadium-style shouting. So then why, you may ask, did God command Abraham to sacrifice his son in the first place?

God is always in pursuit of faith. Without it, the Bible says, we cannot please God.

Can you imagine the pain the Father God went through when His only Son was crying out "My God, My God, why have you forsaken me?" Can you even comprehend the pain Jesus suffered when he was beaten, nailed to a rugged piece of wood, and hung upright to basically suffocate to death on our behalf?

Laying down our lives, pales in comparison. There is nothing we can do BUT to offer ourselves as a sacrifice to God in order for Him to make us worthy enough to be used by Him. This life is fleeting. The Bible calls life a shadow, a phantom. We are here and then we are gone. So, ask yourself this; who can we trust more with our lives, than the One who created us in the first place and then gave His all for us?

Why did I write this book? Because I believe it needed to be written. In my own self, I am nobody. I am an imperfect woman who looks in the mirror every morning and wonders how a God so perfect could love her so much that He was willing to use her despite herself.

Trust me. My mind is officially boggled.

. . .

31

Nehemiah 8:10b (NAS) "...for the joy of the
Lord is your strength."

*Without this, I couldn't have done this life -
you can take that to the bank, cash it in, and
buy a ROLEX!*

Things that baffle me:

1) Women who enjoy house cleaning. I
   mean, seriously?
2) Men who drop their dirty clothes onto the
   floor next to the laundry hamper. Are they
   contemplating whether they can wear
   those jeans one more time, or are they
   anticipating a kangaroo-fetus-moment
   when the Wranglers crawl into the hamper
   by themselves?
3) People who jump from relationship to
   relationship like some sort of hormonal
   hopscotch until they have more notches
   on their belt than Billy the Kid. I mean
   seriously, what are they hoping to find in

the next one? Jesus? Perhaps they should have begun their search with Him in the first place. Hello!

4) Couples who divorce with the excuse that their marriage "ran its course." What does that even mean? Did they enter their union like a race to see who would get to the finish line first? Well, apparently it worked.

5) People who spend fifty-some years roasting every summer in the desert heat without seriously considering moving to a cooler climate. Oh, wait a minute. That's me.

Things that have humbled me:

1) A man I once saw with two prosthetic arms and two prosthetic legs who bypassed the handicap parking space, parked at a distance, and walked hand in hand with his wife into the restaurant like everyone else.

2) A beautiful African American woman named Maggie. After car accidents that resulted in major medical issues and the need for government assistance, she managed to minister to me with a warm smile and encouraging words each time

she entered the lobby of my workplace.
3) Our son and daughter-in-law's perseverance, dedication, and uncompromising love in raising our incredibly special, special needs grandson.
4) Our infant granddaughter as she fought for her life in Phoenix Children's Hospital NICU. And her parents who never let her give up the fight.

Some of my favorite things:

1) A rainy day.
2) A steaming cup of freshly brewed coffee sitting on my nightstand when I wake up in the morning – thanks, Hon. (This is even better on a rainy day.)
3) The first giggle from a grandbaby.
4) Hugs from family members.
5) News of God's favor being poured out onto one of my children.
6) Laughing hysterically with Greg over something silly that one of us did or said. (As we are getting older, this is happening daily.)
7) A conversation with my precious Savior in the middle of the night when no one else is around.
8) Answered prayer.

9) Typing the last period at the end of the final sentence in the last chapter of my book.

THE END

ACKNOWLEDGEMENTS

If I typed out every name of every person who has had some influence on my walk with the Lord, it would be another manuscript. First and foremost, I want to give glory to God! Why God chose me to be His own is beyond comprehension. There is no way I could ever repay Him, and I certainly have never deserved His mercy, grace, or forgiveness. Without Him, I could never have made it through the things of this life that have been much bigger than me.

I want to thank my first husband, Jack, for not only encouraging me to one day write this book, but for being an example of what being Christlike looked like. I want to thank my current husband, Greg, for sticking with me through thick and thin. (Literally, I've been thick and thin.) And for loving me despite the fact that I am still wiggling on the altar.

I want to thank all seven of my children, their spouses, and my grandbabies. You are all the jewels in my crown of life. You each have filled my heart and life with so much joy, encouragement, hope, and love, it is bubbling over.

A special thanks to Joy, my daughter and personal editor, who helped me catch typos. Thanks to my daughter Corissa, for reading this and encouraging me to step out in faith. Thank you, James, my son-in-law, and partner in crime. Your knowledge has helped me steer through the maze of the publishing world for more than one endeavor and I look forward to our partnership in the future.

Thanks to Kathy for pointing me in the right direction when I was veering to the left. Thank you, Linda, and Sue for being the best sisters in the world. And thank you, Mom & Dad, for always encouraging me to use my gifts for the glory of God.

. . .

WIGGLING ON THE ALTAR

WIGGLING ON THE ALTAR